# A Perfect Blend

Stephen D. Redmond

A PERFECT BLEND.

Please direct all copyright inquiries to:

B.O.Y. Publications, Inc.
c/o Author Copyrights
P.O. Box 262
Lowell, NC 28098
betonyourselfent.com

First printing, 2015

Paperback ISBN: 978-1-955605-64-9

Cover and Interior Design: B.O.Y. Enterprises, Inc.

Printed in the United States of America.

# Dedication

I would like to dedicate this book to my children that has been supportive of their father. I know that times were tough and you went without, because of your faithfulness, you will receive your just reward. This book is dedicated to you for all of the nights I was not at home due to football, track season, choir practice, me following our pastor when he preached, or any other endeavor that I was involved in. This book is for Stephen, Stephanie, LaDasia and LaJada. You guys are special and anointed to influence those who are lost and strayed away. You are a Perfect Blend of individuals that bring your own flare and flavor into the world. You are peculiar and royal. You are Perfect in the sight of God because of Jesus Christ. I love you and bless you.

# Acknowledgements

I would like to acknowledge my wife Lady Teresa Redmond who again, inspired me to write a book that will encourage others to pursue what God has for them. Your inspiration and support are like no other. The nights we discuss how to improve our family, church and life push me to be a better husband and leader. You are the perfect example of a help mate. You are and have stayed by my side regardless of what crazy idea that crept in my mind. To acknowledge you in the book is a no brainer and a must. We have some GREAT things to obtain and will obtain them.

# Table of Contents

.

# Foreword

In reading *A Perfect Blend*, you will discover how important a foundation is for your family. How you begin building your family is imperative to the growth and maintenance of a blended family. I know this book will help you identify the foundation, be it good or not so good, that your family is built on. Building a blended family takes love, effort, time, understanding, wisdom, and humility; emerged in faith.

As you dive into the book, you will be advised on how to choose and use your words carefully. Remember life and death are in the power of YOUR tongue. You will be given the tools that we have diligently used and still use to blend our family well. This book isn't rich in your DOs and DON'Ts, but it is saturated in what SHOULD be… THE WORD applied to your family.

What to Expect? Expect to be inspired, equipped challenged and changed after reading *A*

*Perfect Blend.* Read this book with an open mind. See this book through a clear lens. Take the limits off. None of us are perfect, but we strive to be better.

Stephen and I have walked this journey together for 25 years. We beat the odds. We have proved the naysayers wrong. But most of all; we didn't give up on FAMILY. Yes, blended families are successful. Yes, blended families are strong. Yes, blended families are needed. Yes, blended families are REAL FAMILIES!

Sincerely,

Teresa Redmond

# Introduction

As we look at the family structure, it often don't look like what we would think it should. The family that I see now, while I was growing up would be considered dysfunctional. What is dysfunction? This word has led us to believe that it is something without problems, issues, or situations. A dysfunctional family, according to what I was taught from those of the old school, was simply a family that was blended, in chaos, or poor. Well, I guess I am leader of what is considered DYSFUNCTIONAL.

Dysfunction is a word that is often misinterpreted, kind of like the word Christian. Christians believe in Jesus Christ. For many of us that are Christians, we know it is so much more. When looking at the adjective part of speech for the word Christian, it changes the entire context of the word. We now are in the phase in which means to do with Christians or their beliefs. This word Christian becomes life or lifestyle of a number of people describing what we do.

Dysfunction, in reality, is not the picture society paints it to be. The word dysfunction is the deterioration or dwindling of function. This would be a family that is losing its mobility and freedom. This can be if it does not have Kingdom men and women that have the best interest at heart.

In my now 16 years of marriage, many on the outside never knew that my clan, tribe, or household was a dysfunctional household. Just let me stop right now and discontinue calling my family dysfunctional and change the word to BLENDED.

Blended sounds a little better and more like today's lingo. Blended sounds like mixing things, to create or to give flavor. Blending sounds more colorful and exciting and that is what bringing two people together with children from a previous relationship is.

A blended family can be dysfunctional. It can be immobile with no proper working parts or the fading of mobility. It can be many individuals that think of themselves and not of the lives that are at stake. A dysfunctional family is hard to lead, look at, or even talk to because of a bad emotional past.

I will say that the family that I lead does move! It is not immobile. The family at times can be hindered or restricted, but not immobile. It may not move like the average American family, but it moves. Our family moves because of some of the things that we will discuss here in this book. There were some things that God led me, as the leader of my family, to do before I married my beautiful wife Teresa as we brought together with us 3 great children. The children were not all that were brought in.

I also left out some things in this introduction, that sometimes continue to haunt us, but there are other things that were done that make this family stick together through thick and thin. Look at the great assets that your family have and begin speaking life into them and not death. Be the motivator and not the intimidator in your family.

# Chapter 1

## House Construction

### "The Foundation"

**Acts 7:48a (NIV)-** *"However, the Most High does not live in houses made by human hands"*

**Psalms 11:3 (NIV)-** *"When the foundations are being destroyed, what can the righteous do?"*

One day I had the privilege of going to a job site with a friend who builds houses. When we arrived at the house, I saw what looked to be just a wall of concrete. Before he instructed me to get out of the work van, my friend grabbed the plans for the house he was building. As he grabbed the plans, I saw the joy on his face he had for doing something he loved to do. He then told me, "Man you going to love this house." In my thinking at that time, I thought this man has to be crazy for me to be looking at a concrete wall with black waterproof sealant on it. How can I love this house?

We then stepped out of his work van walking in this damp red clay of Anderson, South Carolina. We finally get to the bottom of a hill with a view of Hartwell Lake and step on what I could not see which was the basement of the house. He rolls out the plans; lays them on the ground while grabbing two rocks that would keep the wind from blowing them away. Once the plans were laid out, he reaches in his back pocket and get his tape measurer. He instructs me to grab one end of the tape to help him make sure the measurements are right before the actual house construction. As he discussed measurements, like I really understood what all of that meant, he then talked about how each point and each angle was important. He then stated, "Man for every house, the foundation has to be right. I like crawl spaces. You see, I don't pour slabs unless there is a basement. If you pour a slab and there's is a problem with a slab, you gotta dig it up." I really didn't hear anything past the foundation but remember talking about the crawl space and slabs. The talk about the foundation was why I took that ride to the lake.

In looking at houses, a house can have a huge appreciation of value but if it is built on a slab and that slab cracks, the value of that house is going to depreciate, and the house may fall. How would you like to have to dig up the floor of your house because it is cracked or shifted out of alignment? If digging up the floor is what's needed to be done, maybe that's what we will have to do. Digging up the floor can be expensive! And now I am not just talking about houses. I'm also speaking of families. With any family, you must have a good foundation to avoid costly repairs.

Often times with families, we fail in the area of having a good foundation. A good foundation is not laid because we sometimes find a person that seems to understand our problems; they have met us emotionally and rocked our world in a night of vulnerability. Many people we meet in churches, who seem to be that spiritual partner. The person we encounter often times looks like the fix to the financial problems we have placed ourselves in through careless spending or trying to survive during the hurt of past relationships. Jumping in or from various relationships is not how a good foundation is laid. The foundation must be laid through the conduits of love and communication.

The foundation in blended families can often start out flawed. Some of the flaws can be that one of the other parents does not want someone else raising their child(ren). The Ex can also be jealous or envious about the decision to move on with their child(ren) and without them. Another thing can be the child(ren) does not respect the newly wedded spouse.

If this is the case, there has to be clear communication of respect within the house. Respect is hard within blended families, not only for the children but the adults as well. How do you gain respect? This can be something that is hard to do but obtainable.

First, respect must be gained through communication. In your communication, you cannot be passive. When you or your spouse has agreed to do something, you stick to it and not deter from it. This goes for the other parent(s) and the children. This also is determined on how the previous relationship was with the other parent. How bad was that relationship? Some relationships have been so damaged that there could be danger with you standing your ground. Don't be crazy in your decision making in dealing with your children and your Ex. There must be consistency.

The spirit of consistency can be hard in trying to lay a strong and godly foundation. The key to consistency is having self-control but within having self-control, one must show humility.

**1 Peter 5:6-9 (NIV)-** *Humble yourselves, therefore, under God's mighty hand, that he may lift you up in due time. 7 Cast all your anxiety on him because he cares for you. 8 Be self-controlled and alert. Your enemy the devil prowls around like a roaring lion looking for someone to devour. 9 Resist him, standing firm in the faith, because you know that your brothers throughout the world are undergoing the same kind of suffering."*

In this scripture, being humble is what we must display to show self-control, which is an attribute of the fruit of the Spirit. Displaying any of His fruit shows those around you that you are under the subjection and authority of the Spirit of God. Even though the world may view this as a weakness, things will work out (Romans 8:28). Some may even ask how God is blessing you so when you had children out of wedlock or even divorced which He does not desire. The simple reason is if you have repented and truly confessed, Romans 10:9-10, that you have been saved and redeemed by the blood of Jesus Christ. This is not an easy thing to do but a must. Your life and the life of your family are at stake! This is a FAITH WALK!

*"Do not despise these small beginnings, for the LORD rejoices to see the work begin, to see the plumb line in Zerubbabel's hand."* **- Zechariah 4:10 (NLT)**

Let's go back to the house builder. When we were discussing setting the foundation of the house, my friend stated that he first had to create footers by measuring, placing stakes, and using a plumb. In setting the foundation, the house looked small, insignificant, and undesirable. Remember how I first thought this man was crazy because how excited he was about this big slab of concrete. In my eyes it was nothing, it was small and a big mud mess. The builder saw the finished product. He saw where the sink would be, where the stairs would be placed, and even the placement of the toilet. The beginning of the house was small. The house did not look like it would be over 2000 sq. feet.

The scripture tells us to do the opposite as I did. I despised. Despise is not only to hate but it is to dislike. I did not like what I initially saw. I never said or displayed any emotion, but my thinking was off. My thinking was off because I did not want to, at the time, appreciate the work that seemed so insignificant. Even though I was with him to look at some work he was doing, my wife and I were in discussion of him building us a house. My attitude was off. I had what is considered to be a STANK attitude!

For the builder to use a plumb or plumb line, the fact that he pulled string for the foundation, tells of how meticulous he was in setting the foundation. The builder told me how the plumb helped get every corner of the house even, precise and in line. He stated the plumb line helped him work and walk in excellence.

We must decree and declare that our families walk in excellence. Excellence is not the absence of error, but the mindset you operate in. That's what this verse in Zechariah is telling us. Even though the start of something may seem small and insignificant, God is pleased to see it begin. God is also pleased to see you measure each corner, counting the cost and making sure the foundation is right and able to handle the structure and framework that will be built on it.

You have a house to build that has a foundation that has to be not only laid in excellence but through that conduit of love. The Agape love! The love that is unconditional.

In any relationship we as people place conditions on love. If you buy me that ring, you love me. If you give me the credit card, you love me. If you give me more sex, you love me. If you cook every day, you love me. We can show appreciation this way but is this love? 1Corinthians 13 defines what love is supposed to look like and what is the greatest between faith, hope and love.

As a pastor, I often find myself teaching faith and hope more than love and I see why most of the Body of Christ fails at love. We really don't know what love looks like. Our church services are built on emotions and so are our relationships. So, if everything around us is emotional, that is what our family foundation is, emotional.

The conduit of love does not remind those we love of how bad we felt last week, or the wrong thing said the hour before. We fail our loved ones because of record keeping and our emotional rollercoaster of negative feelings. Most of our negative feelings come from the damage of past relationships that left scars we attempt to cover with harden hearts and harsh speech. So, our conduits are not water pipes that help provide cleanliness, a refreshing or life but sewer pipes that carry the waste of our hurtful experiences.

In Matthew 16:18, Jesus tells Peter "Upon this rock I will build my church; and the gates of hell will not prevail against it." Jesus needed something solid to build on. If the foundation is not solid, the family structure cannot stand.

Even though the concrete slab is a mixture of a rock substance and water it needs water to mix with before it becomes solid. The solidarity of your foundation allows the family structure to stand the test of time. It will allow you to show love no matter if you are going through a prodigal situation (Luke 15:11-32), going through a storm (Mark 4:39), attempt to take a walk of faith (Matthew 14:22-33) or need a healing within the family (Matthew 9:18-26).

Jesus needs something to work with so that He can do His marvelous work. We have all the faith but show little love. We must have a solid foundation so that God can fulfill his promises that he has for our lives.

*"For I know the plans I have for you,"* *declares the LORD,* *"plans to prosper you and not to harm you, plans to give you hope and a future."* **-Jeremiah 29:11 (NIV)**

God has a plan that He has placed you over. He has a building project, and He has made you the foreman, contractor or lead over it. He desires you to build the house and no one can do it like you do. God has a prophet that will give you His word and He is sending His word because He is pleased that you agreed to begin the work. You started something that is not easy, but it will take you being meticulous in getting every corner and edge precise and measured. God has provided grace, mercy, guidance and the anointing for you to get your family in line with His will. All of these things you may not can see. Why not? They are in you. The provision is there, and you just have to believe that God has equipped you. He has equipped you with the vision to see how the family is to run.

God has plans for you and your family. You have to trust the plans He has for you. How do I know His plans? Read His word, meditate on His word, trust His word, speak His word and teach His word.

In knowing His word, you have to sit with your spouse and begin to write what your family is to look like. This is going back to communication. This is the key to what makes any family work. Even though it may be painful, talk about the things that were bad in the previous relationship. Discuss with an open mind to gain understanding of the triggers that may make your spouse relapse or backslide into the hurt person. Remember these to protect them; don't use them to hurt them. To pick at an old wound can infect and affect your marriage and cause distrust within it.

*"Then the Lord replied: "Write down the revelation and make it plain on tablets so that a herald may run with it."* **-Habakkuk 2:2 (NIV)**

Laying the foundation of communication and respect will help you in any relationship. Remember it has to be poured through that conduit of LOVE. Value your marriage and remember the covenant that you have placed with your spouse and God: to love and to cherish, to have and to hold, for better, for worse, for richer, for poorer, in sickness and in health, until death do us part.

These words, I think, have become common and not taken seriously today. I feel that this happens with blended couples, many don't feel they will make it and not take it seriously. You must take your vows seriously and press on for the prize of the higher calling in Christ Jesus. The higher calling is His will and for you to have a blissful marriage.

# Chapter 2

## Being Careful in Dual Meets

### "Judging and Caring"

*"If a house is divided against itself, that house cannot stand. And if Satan opposes himself and is divided, he cannot stand; his end has come. In fact, no one can enter a strong man's house without first tying him up. Then he can plunder the strong man's house."*

**-Mark 3:25-27**

The term dual meets come from, what I feel is the greatest sport in the world, Track and Field. Dual meets or dual competitions take place mainly in the high school arena of the sport. Sometimes these meets can be hard for those who are around the sport 8-9 months a year like I frequently am.

I have the privilege to be the head track coach at Berea High school in Greenville, SC and also be affiliated with the Greenville Jets Track club. My daughter is a member of the Jets and has done very well for herself in a short career. In my affiliation, I am around several athletes from different area schools. For about 5 of those months, I am with the Greenville Jets club, which places me with athlete outside of the team I coach. During track season, sometimes I catch myself coaching and cheering for the Jets kids that run for other high schools. Not saying they aren't important, but I have a team that I am to lead, encourage, and win championships with. They have put their trust in me.

In blended families, we can often find ourselves in the same situation of not cheering but paying attention to the other house or the Ex. Placing our focus on something we have no control over. This can cause friction within the household.

What are some of the things that gain our attention and lose focus on our family? These things could be the children being disrespectful away from our house, a false promise made by the other parent, the lack of child support or parental support, the Ex bringing up the past, speaking to the Ex in private, not communicating with your spouse when the Ex calls, being alone with the Ex, allowing your children to disrespect your spouse, and raising the children separately.

Cheering for the other team or paying too much attention to the other team brings MUCH conflict. How does this happen, you may ask? The conversation tends to be about the other person and you taking their side when difficult situations arise. This can cause a house to be divided.

In Matthew 3, Jesus is using the illustration of a house divided. In the case of coaching, there is a divided mindset toward the athletes seen during the summer and those that I am responsible for. I can speak to them, acknowledge them and respect them but coaching them and giving them my undivided attention is disrespectful to my team. Those athletes have a coach, even if I do not agree with how they are coached; I am being careless and disrespectful to my team during the dual meet.

Here is some helpful advice! In Track and Field, dual meets don't matter as much as a football, baseball, or basketball competition. Team wins and losses are kept track of but not equated during the Championship part of the season. The thing a good track coach looks for in dual meets is progress. Progress is most important. The coach should make sure the athletes are consistent and they are on track to making it to the next level of competition which is called advancing. Some meets, a coach just may want to work on specific things.

As a leader of a family, winning that argument with the Ex, just by having the last word, cussing them out to be the one on top or just seeming that you are the winner should not be the goal. You must make sure that in every situation and circumstance you are making progress. Even though the other parent or child may know your weakness, allow God to be your strength in that area. Depend on His teaching and connect to a great teaching ministry in your city or area.

In getting connected to a good teaching ministry, that ministry will encourage you to learn and study more. The growth will challenge you and make you bold in the word of God. Also getting connected to true children of God does the same thing to the mind and soul. The Bible calls this, to hunger and thirst after righteousness. Since I am a track coach, this would be me encouraging good hydration and diet to maximize peak performance.

Jesus uses, in Mark 3, a reference of a strong man. Jesus stated that no man can enter a strong man's house unless first tying him up. In the case of my coaching, I was being tied up because of the way I treated my team. You are tied up by having your focus on things you cannot control. If you disagree with how your children treat someone else, especially the other parent, handle that on your time and not the other parent's time. Encourage respect.

Many Exes love to take the spotlight. Some are intentional and other may not be intentional. That may be a weakness that they have. We all have weaknesses. Only handle what you can handle. You be the godly example that your kids should see. As my mother-in-law says, "Time will tell!" Time will tell if this is an intentional thing to get your attention. Attention seeking is a very dangerous thing to do.

> *"Because of the LORD's great love we are not consumed, for his compassions never fail. They are new every morning; great is your faithfulness."*
> **-Lamentations 3:22**

Track and Field is so much different than most team sports. In track, many of the athletes like to get in races that they know can be won easily and attempt to judge others based on what was done the meet before. The only thing about that is this sport is solely based on top performance on that particular day not because you won a heat.

The difference between God and track is that He does not base things on our performance because He performs the good work, (Philippians 1:6). He just wants us to get up, get ready, and compete in the race to the best of our ability. Our top performance may not equal someone else's, but God wants our best. Recognize what your best is and do that.

Know what the best is in your house. Judging what the Ex has done, what my child is compared to yours is not healthy in the blended family or any family. We must teach them according to the word of God and their ability. What does the word say? What can they do well? Identify the problem your spouse and my children have and coach them up. Teach them! If they are falling short in an area, let's make them stronger.

*"But he said to me, "My grace is sufficient for you, for my power is made perfect in weakness." Therefore I will boast all the more gladly about my weaknesses, so that Christ's power may rest on me. 10 That is why, for Christ's sake, I delight in weaknesses, in insults, in hardships, in persecutions, in difficulties. For when I am weak, then I am strong."*
**-2 Corinthians 12:9-10**

One thing that we often do is not pay attention to our weakness. In coaching, it is the opposite, we look at our weaknesses very often. Not saying that our weakness will be equal to our strength but to be better at our weakness so that it will not be so noticeable. Everybody has a weakness; every team, every organization, every family and everything has a weakness, and they must be addressed. In addressing the weakness, it must be done through the word of God. That's where the power comes from that activated the grace that Paul is writing about in 2 Corinthians 12.

This place we often shy away from, our weakness. Paul tells us to delight in weakness. This is a place where it's uncomfortable. This is a place, weakness, where most people like to dwell and stay and remind that I'm not good enough. Not their own weakness, my weakness. When I am aware of my weakness but confident in my strong areas, the word can keep guard in the area of my weakness. That's why we must delight there.

No family has it all together, blended or not. The key is acknowledging where you are weak. If you know your spouse is weak in money, they should not handle the finances. As said in the hood, "You do you!" Know your weaknesses, address them, strengthen them in the word, and let's have better families.

In coaching, I had a problem of dealing with outside athletes and not completely dealing with the athletes I had, during the meets. Since I coach sprint/relays, I wanted good sprint/relays and would satisfy that by encouraging athletes from other teams. I did coach my athletes in practice but the satisfaction of having ties to a team that was where I wanted mine to be, this caused dysfunction within the camp. Not major dysfunction but dysfunction is just what it is. My need to be successful overtook my priority to make what I had better. I compared the goods. Comparing the goods is a MAJOR mistake in any relationship.

*"Simon, Simon, Satan has asked to sift each of you as wheat."* **-Luke 22:31 (NIV)**

When we compare goods and do not deal with weaknesses, this causes discord and separation within the family. When we have discord and separation this is exactly what the enemy desires. When we are separated we are no longer tight and able to impact others that are assigned to us. We are no longer able to obtain the promises that God has for us. We can obtain them but tend to cause more frustration in our lives because we feel God is holding them from us but wondering in the wilderness of doubt, self-pity and strife. We are being sifted!

When we are sifted, we are usually being selfish and want to be right. We want everything to go our way and don't care about anyone else. I was that way in coaching. I feel that I'm a good coach but because I was starting over and building a program again, I wanted things to be like it was when I was head coach previously, all things in order, and all the kids coming out because I speak into them and build relationships. However, I needed to recognize I was starting over!

In most blended families that's what we are doing, starting over but with added ingredients. The other ingredients are as important. There are other people involved in the process of starting over. The kids are comparing you to their parents and sometimes your spouse compares you to the old relationship. Is it fair? No, but it happens.

## How do we deal with the weakness?

First, we must praise the good. In praising the good, we are giving something that everyone wants, praise and acknowledgement! Praise and acknowledgement are the components of the bridge that helps get to the next thing.

Secondly, we must admit there is bad. This is confession. In the previous chapter, we briefly talked about Roman 10:9. If we never confess, we never get better. If we never confess, we can never delight in our weaknesses. Delight is protection. How is it protection? When we delight, we shed light on what is dark. When we shed light, this keeps us from stumbling in that area of weakness. Our weaknesses are the dark areas of our lives. Alcoholics Anonymous believes in confessing, why can't we?

Once we deal with at least these two areas, we can start to move on as a family. Not just that of the blended variety. These things help us grow not only as Christians but leaders, families and business owners. What are the weaknesses? Be careful in the dual meet! These are the places that we compete but looking to progress in the faith and in life. We are not trying to prove who is better which at times manipulate our children, spouses, and others. We are trying to get better through Christ. We are always in a battle, competition, or fight. These things are to make us strong and to enhance us in our walk with Christ.

# Chapter 3

## Expectations and Limits

### "Your Reality"

*"So the man gave them his attention, expecting to get something from them."* **-Acts 3:5**

In today's society, the rule of expectation is used but the willingness to work is ignored. Many people today want something for nothing. In that mindset, a person sets themselves up to be disappointed or take it upon themselves to forcefully take what they want. This mind set has destroyed many lives and still is destroying today.

During my childhood, I remember many parents saying a simple phrase that I believe got us in this place that we are in. Many parents would say, "I want my children to have the things I never had." When they got what they never had, those children missed the things that they did have. Those things were love, attention, discipline, and being taught how to show respect. Now they were missing some other things but those are some of the most important things that children need.

With that being said, I saw many in my generation get things that were ridiculous in price. I remember that my parents along with a few others decided that it was time for us to get money for Christmas. The parents grew tired of doing all of that shopping only for their children to complain about things being too small and not big enough. We were the generation that began the sagging pants. Once we received our money, we headed to the mall to do some shopping. I never will forget that time. During that time $200.00, along with smart shopping, you could really buy a lot.

Once we got to the mall, two of us decided we would look to see what sales were going on and a friend of ours wanted to go to "Rich's" to get some Polo. We encouraged him to shop around first, but he wanted that Polo from "Rich's".

After browsing for some time, he caught back up with us. He mentioned that he was ready to go, but we had only purchased a few items. He was excited and showed us what he bought. In his bag he had 2 shirts and a pair of jeans that cost him $130.00 of his $140.00. He then got mad at us because we were not ready and still looking in various stores for deals.

While we continued to look and he grew more impatient, so he decided to go get a pair of socks that were on sale for $7.00 which left him with $3.00. My other friend and I were still shopping finding deals and purchasing outfits instead of a few items. Once we were finished, we all wanted something to eat. We all had money, but one did not have enough to purchase a good meal. You know how things get with teenagers. It was not pretty! An argument brewed because we were wrong for shopping smart.

In this illustration, all three of us were able to do all of the same things. I did not mention that all of our parents told us to shop smart and what to look for. We were all given expectations. We were expected to shop smart and come home with multiple things, outfits. Within the day we did meet the expectations but had no limits. Two of us met the expectation and one of us didn't.

Within all of our families we have expectations but most of the time there are no limits. We expect our family to love, expect our family to respect, and expect others to be there for one another. What are our expectations built on? Where do we get these expectations from?

Our expectations come mainly because that's our family. How do we know what is expected if there is never conversation about the subject? What does expectation look like within a family?

During the time I shopped with my friends, our parents told us all to shop smart. We never were told how to shop smart but two of us had an idea what that was while the other thought it was getting a certain name brand. Once we returned home, we all understood what shopping smart was. Hindsight is 20/20! It was to get a good deal and to seek out sales. Our parents did not want us to pay full price. The one friend thought he was shopping smart. He didn't pay full price! He did pay a large price! He thought he met the expectation.

Sitting down and discussing expectations is a healthy but often uncomfortable thing to do for all families. In blended families it is extremely important. Each family member needs to understand what is expected from them and what the expectation looks like.

Explaining expectations tells all parties involved, the spouse, ex, children and grandparents what to expect in the family. What the family will look like at a certain point. It tells everyone what it is supposed to be in the end… the desired end!

In my family, my wife and I discussed this before we got married. We talked about visitations, holidays, discipline, church, and money. We set what we expected with all of these topics. The expectations were set so everyone would know the outcome; the limitations are as equally important to.

In the example of my friends and I shopping experience, we met the expectation of our parents, but limits were never set or explained. We were never told exactly what to look for. How my one friend and I understood our limits was because we paid attention while shopping in times past with our parents. We saw how our parents clipped coupons and went from store to store shopping for the best deals. We paid close attention to how our parents saved and purchased what was needed for our houses. What we needed was multiple shirts, multiple pants, and other items not the top fashion. The limits were set from past experiences not conversation. Our parents set an EXAMPLE.

Even though expectations are in place you have to set limits. Limits tell how high or low something will go spiritually and emotionally. Because there is a past relationship, the Ex really knows more about your spouse than you do. If not know them better, they know what buttons to push to start either or both of you on an emotional tailspin. That tailspin can get you like in the previous chapter, paying more attention to them than what is at home. Having no limits may make others think they can treat you and play with your emotions like they used to. Things are emotional enough. You are going through a major adjustment in your life. You brought together many different worlds under one roof and are expecting everyone to get along. Why not set limits?

*"What good is it, my brothers, if someone says he has faith but does not have works? Can that faith save him? If a brother or sister is poorly clothed and lacking in daily food, and one of you says to them, "Go in peace, be warmed and filled," without giving them the things needed for the body, what good[a] is that? So also faith by itself, if it does not have works, is dead. But someone will say, "You have faith and I have works." Show me your faith apart from your works, and I will show you my faith by my works. You believe that God is one; you do well. Even the demons believe—and shudder! Do you want to be*

*shown, you foolish person, that faith apart from works is useless?"* **-James 2:14-20 (ESV)**

Even though we discuss limits, what you show is more important than what you say. In telling someone what you will not take and only complaining, arguing and making idle threats, will never get you to the next place God has for you and your family. God has expectations and limits: In Galatians 6:9 Paul writes, "at the right time we will reap a harvest of blessings if we do no give up." The expectation is the harvest, and the limit is if we do not give up.

Giving up on our families should not be an option. Our hearts desire should be to; stand firm, hold your position and see the salvation of the Lord (2 Chronicle 20:17a). Our stance tells where our faith is, and our faith shows our position. Our positions should display our expectations for our family which is salvation.

The desired end of all we do and teach our families should lead towards salvation. Salvation is the saving power of Jesus Christ through the shedding of his blood on Calvary. Our position should be that of the cross which is the example of the relationship between God and man along with man and the rest of humanity. The humanity that we first must have is a relationship with those in our homes, FAMILY. Our relationship outside our family should not be better than inside the home. Like in the previous chapter, pay more attention to the house and spouse than we do any outside relationship. This can be avoided by setting expectations and limitations. Our expectations are set in scripture like Jeremiah 29:11 and our limits are set in Galatians 6:9.

When we set limits and expectations, the order of our house will be in place. For business individuals, you can also think of this as a mission statement and purpose. Once these are in existence everyone involves knows what to do and how it should be done. Set these in place and watch your family understand their purpose.

# Chapter 4

## Intimidation of Independence

### "Staying Out Of Isolation"

*"The LORD God said, "It is not good for the man to be alone. I will make a helper suitable for him."* **-Genesis 2:18**

One of the most intimidating things for others about a person can be their independence. Independence is something that we all desire to have, but that very thing can be the tree that we eat from that spirals us into the depths and darkness of sin. That is the fruit that causes us to want to know those things that God rather us not experience yet because of our immaturity. Our immaturity can be the craftiness of our thinking that often tells us that the unknown is alright for us to gain knowledge of.

In looking at the fall of man, many of us like to blame Adam for not being in his place as the man when he left Eve alone with the serpent. In Genesis 2:19, God brought the animals to Adam to see what he would name them. There was a relationship between God, man, and the creatures that God created. There was nothing uncommon for the animals or creeping things to be around both Adam and Eve. There was dominion that man had in the garden. That dominion placed control over everything that was in the garden that God made. Dominion is also where the word dominate came from. No one could overthrow Adam but he could set himself back.

Setbacks usually come from emotional thinking. Emotional thinking can be the start of knowing good and evil; we know the good of a thing and the bad of it. This thought process often causes us to not totally commit to something. Wrong or negative emotions can cause premature break-ups of potential God-connected relationships and marriages.

Many marriages are lost because no clear authority has been defined or one person finds themselves out of line and out of order. The biblical order of marriage is husband and then wife. This is not to be mistaken as the husband dominates the wife. Here is one problem. Most men do not understand what a husband is!

One of the defined meanings of Husband is to till or cultivate. When a man tills and cultivates his family, he is preparing them by using the right words that are sown in his family's mind. He is producing after his own kind. The husband has to break the fallow ground of negative thinking and reassure his wife that he is the head and will be the provider that God is for him.

If the man never understands the role, many wives will never fall in line and truly submit. The lack of submitting causes the woman to remain independent which keeps the man always seeking authority and feeling less than a man. This less than feeling can cause dissention, withdrawal, stress, and anger while looking for validation in the wrong places. If the man or woman does not get affirmed or validated, the will to be independent will be the strength of the marriage and the two will never become ONE!

When speaking of TWO, that is a sign of INDEPENDENCE! We as a nation have a Declaration of Independence and most couples have the same mindset and declare their independence. We are declaring we are separate from the Kingdom of structure and order. This never allows us to come into true covenant agreement with God or the family we have joined. God never told us to declare independence. What we must declare is the glory that the Heavens declared, Psalms 19:1. God declares His covenant which is the Ten Commandments, as referenced in Deuteronomy 4:13.

If God declares His covenant, why can't we declare the covenant that we made with God, our spouse, family, church, and community? We often declare our independence that keeps us buried in the sin of deception resulting in unhealthy relationships that damage not only us, but the children brought in the relationship.

Children are looking for discipline, covenant, and structure but we as married people, sometimes never submit to the will of God nor rely on His spirit which dwells in His word. We rely on the pastor to articulate what they have to say about issues and subjects that should be researched in alone time with the presence of God. God never intended on us being independent in any area of our lives. He made Adam a help meet which caused him to have to lean on another being. He created Adam to have dominion. Does that imply he did not need help with something?

Even when Adam named the animals, God wanted to see what he would name them. This shows that man had the freedom to call each fowl, creeping thing and beast whatever he wanted. Yet, even with the power to name, God oversaw what Adam was doing in that moment of calling those things what they were about to be.

*"So the Lord God formed from the ground all the wild animals and all the birds of the sky. He brought them to the man to see what he would call*

*them, and the man chose a name for each one."* - **Genesis 2:19**

If we begin to view the creation of man and woman as more than just gender, we could see that the fall of man was not solely based on gender. Let's look at man being the authority of humankind with woman being the emotion of humankind. These two things are placed in each person that walks here on the earth. Many people let their emotions control their thinking, feelings, career, and path in life. Many are waiting to feel stirred up before they can move on anything. Waiting on things to be stirred keeps us relying on ourselves, outside forces, or other people. This is a flesh centered mindset.

*"Sir, the invalid replied, "I have no one to help me into the pool when the water is stirred. While I am trying to getting, someone else goes down ahead of me."* **-John 5:7**

The human race had one problem and that was humans knew what God knew. With knowing what God knows, we often think we are independent of God. The serpent's craftiness caused a desire for man to be equal with God. This desire was done through the emotions of man. The woman! Again, woman not a gender, but the part that came from your rib that connects to the nerves of the spine.

*"or because of these surpassingly great revelations. Therefore, in order to keep me from becoming conceited, I was given a thorn in my flesh, a messenger of Satan, to torment me."* **-2 Corinthians 12:7**

The thorns we have in our lives, these nagging prickly pieces, keep us humble and not conceited. They keep us dependent, most of all, on God and spouses who are our helpers in this walk called life. We all have a place of authority. We all have places or gifts where we flourish but in constant need of assistance to reach the goal of having dominion. In having dominion, we must be fruitful, multiply, fill the earth and subdue (overcome).

In reaching these 4 mandates we need help in the multiplication process. Humans are not asexual! A man needs a woman to add to humanity and vice versa. The nurturer or mother is needed to help balance the discipline that the father brings.

There are so many examples that can be brought out on the dependency of mankind. One of the major issues that we face is that we all think we know what is best for us but usually experience the worst, GOOD and EVIL. When good and evil are experienced or we know what's good and feel the results of evil, we are usually in a state of loneliness and despair. The loneliness we feel is most often the result in us hiding ourselves instead of going to the One who gave us instructions in our places of dominion. We become independent as Adam and Eve did in the garden by eating the fruit of the tree of knowledge of good and evil.

Our willingness to know or have knowledge is often intimidating to our spouses, friends, family, and friends. Knowing causes independence. Knowing what is good or good for us causes demands to be placed on our families.

These demands generally lead to selfishness. Our selfishness most often causes loneliness. Loneliness is often felt in marriages.

Our independence can cause us to be separate entities even in marriage. Independence often intimidates those who are looking at how we live, act, and commune with others. Do you isolate yourself from your spouse by your actions?

I know you have done this thing on your own for years, but you now have a help meet. Help meet or Help mates help you reach the destination for your life. If you could do it alone, you would have already done it. Instead, you decided to marry and be in this blended family, this family not produced by the same people but now raised by the two that are now joined. This can be a potential train wreck that could happen if divine order is not placed in the home of mixed children, personalities, and bloodlines.

Order is structure that should be placed for a home to be successful. Just like in the previous chapter of this book, all involved in this should know what is expected in your house and no one is allowed to be isolated or independent to the call and the will of God for the family. When one is called, all are called!

You may never know that the order you set for your house could be the very thing that blesses your Ex and causes them to get in alignment with the will of God. Someone is always watching!

Stay away from independence and get in the dependence of the will of God. The will of God is your dependence on God. Your independence does not only intimidate others but later intimidates you through isolation and abandonment!

# About the Author

Stephen D. Redmond is a founding member of The Change Church in Greenville, SC. He founded and pastor Turning Point Outreach in Greenville. He attended Greenville Technical college and Anderson University in Anderson, SC. He is an accomplished musician, song-writer and composer that has served in many functions in the Upstate of South Carolina. He is also a Behavior Interventionist in the Greenville County School District. He has coached football, cross country, and track and field in the school district for over 25 years.

He is married to the former Teresa Byers, and they have four children: Stephanie, Stephen "Duke," Ladasia, and Jada.


Contact information:
PST Ministries
(864) 649-0159
Email: yetpraisehim@yahoo.com

Follow us on Twitter:
StephenRedmond

Like us on Facebook:
PSTMinistries